365 Inspirational Quotes

Daily Motivational Quotes

Reach Your Full Potential

Increase Productivity and

Positive Thinking

Amelia Sealey

© Copyright 2021 - All rights reserved.

You may not reproduce, duplicate or send the contents of this book without direct written permission from the author. You cannot hereby despite any circumstance blame the publisher or hold him or her to legal responsibility for any reparation, compensations, or monetary forfeiture owing to the information included herein, either in a direct or an indirect way.

Legal Notice: This book has copyright protection. You can use the book for personal purpose. You should not sell, use, alter, distribute, quote, take excerpts or paraphrase in part or whole the material contained in this book without obtaining the permission of the author first.

Disclaimer Notice: You must take note that the information in this document is for casual reading and entertainment purposes only.
We have made every attempt to provide accurate, up to date and reliable information. We do not express or imply guarantees of any kind. The persons who read admit that the writer is not occupied in giving legal, financial, medical or other advice. We put this book content by sourcing various places.

Please consult a licensed professional before you try any techniques shown in this book. By going through this document, the book lover comes to an agreement that under no situation is the author accountable for any forfeiture, direct or indirect, which they may incur because of the use of material contained in this document, including, but not limited to, — errors, omissions, or inaccuracies.

Are you looking for the best inspirational quotes? Over the years I've collected 365 of the best quotes to motivate and inspire you throughout the year.

These wise and beautiful words from your favorite positive thinkers will put you in the right frame of mind to face whatever obstacles lie ahead. Inspirational quotes from successful people can help you reframe negative thoughts during difficult times and change your attitude so you feel refreshed and motivated. Whether you hope to achieve success at work, at home or in life in general, setting the right intentions can help you stay positive and optimistic during the challenges that fate may throw your way.

No matter what you're feeling or experiencing, we hope these inspirational quotes can help you get to where you want to be.

1. "Give up defining yourself – to yourself or to others. You won't die. You will come to life. And don't be concerned with how others define you. When they define you, they are limiting themselves, so it's their problem. Whenever you interact with people, don't be there primarily as a function or a role, but as the field of conscious Presence. You can only lose something that you have, but you cannot lose something that you are." – **Eckhart Tolle**

2. "When you let go of the belief that you should or need to know who you are, what happens to confusion? Suddenly it is gone. When you fully accept that you don't know, you actually enter a state of peace and clarity that is closer to who you truly are than thought could ever be. Defining yourself through thought is limiting yourself." – **Eckhart Tolle**

3. "Faith is the substance of whatever it is that we hope for. The important thing is that we teach that faith is connected to goof works and responsibility."
–Eckhart Tolle

4. "All negativity is caused by an accumulation of psychological time and denial of the present. Unease, anxiety, tension, stress, worry – all forms of fear – are caused by too much future, and not enough presence. Guilt, regret, resentment, grievances, sadness, bitterness, and all forms of nonforgiveness are caused by too much past, and not enough presence." – **Eckhart Tolle**

5. "The moment you realize you are not present, you are present. Whenever you are able to observe your mind, you are no longer trapped in it. Another factor has come in, something that is not of the mind: the witnessing presence." – **Eckhart Tolle**

6. "Physical reality is only a mirror. And whatever you define it to be; whatever you believe is most true, is what you get. So it's very important to pay attention to those beliefs and those definitions, for it is those and only those that create your physical reality experience." – **Bashar**

7. "The purpose of a relationship is to reflect to all the others in the relationship what they need to

understand to become more of themselves. Everyone in a relationship is in a relationship for the purpose of helping the other people in the relationship, giving them opportunities to learn to be who they are more and more."
– **Bashar**

8. "The greatest gift creation has given to all of you is that life is fundamentally meaningless. That means it has no built-in meaning. What that also means is, you were designed to give it the meaning you prefer to give it. And the meaning you give it will utterly

determine how you experience it."
— **Bashar**

9. "You know why it's hard to be happy—it's because we refuse to LET GO of the things that make us sad." — **Bruce H. Lipton**

10. "Our beliefs control our bodies, our minds, and thus our lives..."
–**Bruce H. Lipton**

11. "We are not victims of our genes, but masters of our fates, able to create lives overflowing with peace, happiness, and love."
— **Bruce H. Lipton**

12. "At the atomic level, matter does not even exist with certainty; it only exists as a tendency to exist." – **Bruce H. Lipton**

13. "Do what is easy and your life will be hard. Do what is hard and your life will become easy. When your why is big enough you will find your how. You gotta be hungry. The greatest revenge is massive success. You are the only real obstacle in your path to fulfilling it." – **Les Brown**

14. "No matter how bad it is or how bad it gets I am going to make it. If you take responsibility for yourself you will develop a hunger to accomplish your dreams. The easiest thing I ever did was earn a million dollars. The hardest thing I ever did, and it took years, was believing I was capable of earning a million dollars. As you reach your goals set new ones. That is how you grow and become a more powerful person. Help others achieve their dreams and you will achieve yours. " – **Les Brown**

15. "You will win if you don't quit. You cannot expect to achieve new goals or move beyond your present circumstances unless you change. When life knocks you down, try to land on your back. Because if you can look up, you can

get up. Let your reason get you back up.
Forgive yourself for your faults and your mistakes and move on. Too many of us are not living our dreams because we are living our fears." — **Les Brown**

16. "Your life right now is a reflection of your past thoughts. That includes all the great things, and all the things you consider not so great. Since you attract to you what you think about most, it is easy to see what your dominant thoughts have been on every subject of your life, because that is what you have experienced. Until now!" — **Rhonda Byrne**

17. "Everything else you see and experience in this world is effect, and that includes your feelings. The cause is always your thoughts." – **Rhonda Byrne**

18. "Life doesn't just happen to you; you receive everything in your life based on what you've given."
–**Rhonda Byrne**

19. "There are two things you need if you are to uncover and communicate what is really happening in the world. One is to free of any dogmatic belief system. The second is not to give a damn what people think and say about you, or, at least, not to let that influence your decisions." – **David Icke**

20. "The human race is a herd. Here we are, unique, eternal aspects of consciousness with an infinity of potential, and we have allowed ourselves to become an unthinking, unquestioning blob of conformity and uniformity. A herd. Once we concede to the herd mentality, we can be controlled and directed by a tiny few. And we are." – **David Icke**

21. "Dogmas take endless forms, and when you can persuade different people to hold opposing dogmas, the manipulation of conflict and control through "divide and rule" becomes easy. It

is happening today in the same way - more so, in fact - as it has throughout human history."
—**David Icke**

22. "The best way of removing negativity is to laugh and be joyous." – **David Icke**

23. "Experience life in all possible ways -- good-bad, bitter-sweet, dark-light, summer-winter. Experience all the dualities. Don't be afraid of experience, because the more experience you have, the more mature you become." – **Osho**

24. "Sadness gives depth. Happiness gives height. Sadness gives roots. Happiness gives branches. Happiness is like a tree going into the sky, and sadness is like the roots going down into the womb of the earth. Both are needed, and the higher a tree goes, the deeper it goes, simultaneously. The bigger the tree, the bigger will be its roots. In fact, it is always in proportion. That's its balance." – **Osho**

25. "Be — don't try to become. To be creative means to be in love with life. You can be creative only if you love life enough that you want to enhance its beauty, you want to bring a little more music to it, a little more poetry to it, a little more dance to it." – **Osho**

26. "Friendship is the purest love. It is the highest form of Love where nothing is asked for, no condition, where one simply enjoys giving." — **Osho**

27. "The ability to observe without evaluating is the highest form of intelligence." — **J. Krishnamurti**

28. "You must understand the whole of life, not just one little part of it. That is why you must read, that is why you must look at the skies, that is why you must sing, and dance, and write poems, and suffer, and understand, for all that is life." — **Jiddu Krishnamurti**

29. "Freedom and love go together. Love is not a reaction. If I love you because you love me, that is mere trade, a thing to be bought in the market; it is not love. To love is not to ask anything in return, not even to feel that you are giving something- and it is only such love that can know freedom." – **J. Krishnamurti**

30."If you accept a limiting belief, then it will become a truth for you. The thoughts we choose to think are the tools we use to paint the canvas of our lives. I do not fix problems. I fix my thinking. Then problems fix themselves. Every thought we think is creating our future." – **Louise Hay**

31."The past has no power over us. It doesn't matter how long we have had a negative pattern. The point of power is in the present moment. What a wonderful thing to realize! We can begin to be free in this moment!" — **Louise Hay**

32."If I want to be accepted as I am, then I need to be willing to accept others as they are. When there is a problem, there is not something to do, there is something to know. Every Experience is a Success." — **Louise Hay**

33."Eternity is not endless time, eternity means timeless." — **Mooji**

34."Throw everything away, forget about it all! You are learning too much, remembering too much, trying too hard . . . relax a little bit, give life a chance to flow its own way, unassisted by your mind and effort. Stop directing the river's flow." – **Mooji**

35. "Whatever comes, don't push it away. When it goes, do not grieve." – **Mooji**

36. "Dying to your own attachments is a beautiful death. Because this death release you into real life. You have to die as a seed to live as a tree." – **Mooji**

37. "Feelings are just visitors, let them come and go." – **Mooji**

38. "Surrounded by nothingness you have to do nothing. You have to do nothing to be who you are. Nothing at all." – **Sri H.W.L. Poonja**

39. "Let your will burn in this fire so that it takes you nowhere else. Let your self be burned in this fire of eternity, love and peace. Don't be afraid of this fire, it is love itself. This desire for freedom is the fire of love!" – **H.W.L. Poonja**

40. "One is always free and one is always alone. The mind is only dreaming." – **H.W.L. Poonja**

41. "If there is peace in your mind, you will find peace with everybody. If your mind is agitated, you will find agitation everywhere. So first find peace within and you will see this inner peace reflected everywhere else. Where else will you find peace if not within you?"
– **H.W.L. Poonja**

42. "The way to live a happy beautiful life is to accept whatever comes and not care about what does not come." – **H.W.L. Poonja**

43. "To let life happen to you is irresponsible. To create your day is your divine right." – **Ramtha**

44. "Face your fears and allow yourself to unmask their illusion." – **Ramtha**

45. "As long as you accept only those limited thoughts that have been bred into you, you will never activate greater portions of your brain to receive and experience any thought other than what you have faced every day of your existence." – **Ramtha**

46. "You know, it is very simple to be a genius. All you have to do is think for yourself." – **Ramtha**

47. "If you believe it will work out, you'll see opportunities. If you believe it won't you will see obstacles." – **Dr. Wayne Dyer**

48. "Change the way you look at things and the things you look at change." – **Dr. Wayne Dyer**

49. "With everything that has happened to you, you can feel sorry for yourself or treat what has happened as a gift. Everything is either an opportunity to grow or an obstacle to keep you from growing. You get to choose."
–**Dr. Wayne Dyer**

50. "Go for it now. The future is promised to no one." – **Dr. Wayne Dyer**

51. "Life begins at the end of your comfort zone." – **Neale Donald Walsch**

52. "The deepest secret is that life is not a process of discovery, but a process of creation. You are not discovering yourself, but creating yourself anew. Seek therefore, not to find out Who You Are, but seek to determine Who You Want to Be." – **Neale Donald Walsch**

53. "If you want the best the world has to offer, offer the world your best." – **Neale Donald Walsch**

54. "To be empowered—to be free, to be unlimited, to be creative, to be genius, to be divine—that is who you are…. Once you feel this way, memorize this feeling; remember this feeling. This is who you really are…." – **Joe Dispenza**

55. "If you want a new outcome, you will have to break the habit of being yourself, and reinvent a new self." – **Joe Dispenza**

56. "So if we want to change some aspect of our reality, we have to think, feel, and act in new ways; we have to "be" different in terms of our responses to experiences. We have to "become" someone else. We have to create a new state of mind … we need to observe a new outcome with that new mind." – **Joe Dispenza**

57. "People mistakenly assume that their thinking is done by their head; it is actually done by the heart which first dictates the conclusion, then commands the head to provide the reasoning that will defend it." – **Anthony de Mello**

58. "When you get rid of your fear of failure, your tensions about succeeding... you can be yourself. Relaxed. You'll no longer be driving with your brakes on." – **Anthony De Mello**

59. "Don't ask the world to change....you change first."
–**Anthony de Mello**

60. "Integrity Is The Most Valuable And Respected Quality Of

Leadership. Always Keep Your Word." – **Brian Tracy**

61. "Leadership Is The Ability To Get Extraordinary Achievement From Ordinary People" – **Brian Tracy**

62. "Leaders Think And Talk About The Solutions. Followers Think And Talk About The Problems." – **Brian Tracy**

63. '' Quality means doing it right when no one is looking.'' – **Henry Ford**

64. '' So there's a kind of resurgence of the sense of freedom and spontaneity in nature. From nature being bound into a rigid, deterministic model, freedom, spontaneity and openness are emerging once again. It's now recognized the future is open, not determined by the past. And this is true in many realms, the astronomical realm, the human realm, the meteorological realm in many ways." – **Rupert Sheldrake**

65. "Not every good idea survives. Not every new form of art is repeated. Not every new potential instinct is successful. Only the successful ones get repeated. By natural selection and then through repetition they become probable, more habitual." – **Rupert Sheldrake**

66. "Remember, all the answers you need are inside of you; you only have to become quiet enough to hear them." – **Debbie Ford**

67. "Your life will be transformed when you make peace with your shadow. The caterpillar will become a breathtakingly beautiful butterfly. You will no longer have to pretend to be someone you're not. You will no longer have to prove you're good enough. When you embrace your shadow you will no longer have to life in fear. Find the gifts of your shadow and you will finally revel in all the glory of your true self. Then you will have the freedom to create the life you have always desired." – **Debbie Ford**

68. "The greatest act of courage is to be and to own all of who you are — without apology, without excuses, without masks to cover the truth of who you are." – **Debbie Ford**

69. "Every time you are tempted to react in the same old way, ask if you want to be a prisoner of the past or a pioneer of the future." – **Deepak Chopra**

70. "You must find the place inside yourself where nothing is impossible." – **Deepak Chopra**

71. "The Ego, however, is not who you really are. The ego is your self-image; it is your social mask; it is the role you are playing. Your social mask thrives on approval. It wants control, and it is sustained by power, because it lives in fear." – **Deepak Chopra**

72. "There is so much good in the worst of us, and so much bad in the best of us, it doesn't behove any of us to speak evil of the rest of us" – **Edgar Cayce**

73. "A soulmate is an ongoing connection with another individual that the soul picks up again in various times and places over lifetimes. We are attracted to another person at a soul level not because that person is our unique complement, but because by being with that individual, we are somehow provided with an impetus to become whole ourselves." – **Edgar Cayce**

74. "Dreams are today's answers to tomorrow's questions." – **Edgar Cayce**

75. "When we open ourselves to experience the true magic and the

pure heart, that lies behind so many cultures, we can go beyond prejudice, limitation and fear, for deep within the human heart is a natural rhythm of harmony that is longing to be released."
–**Jasmuheen**

76."Asking and being open to receive is one of the first steps required to receive some of the gifts of the quantum field. Taking control via our lifestyle to tune to specific channels within the universal field is a basic and easy art to learn." – **Jasmuheen**

77."I have found that when we celebrate our differences we unify with each other in a field of appreciation that is unparallel to the alternative we have known – the field of gossip and judgment which can perpetuate loneliness and separation.

When we seek to understand what another appreciates about their own way of life, and when we take the chance to see their life and the beauty of their culture though their eyes, this action and choice can eliminate feelings of both fear and separation and bond us deeply." – **Jasmuheen**

78. "Change your conception of yourself and you will automatically change the world in which you live. Do not try to change people; they are only messengers telling you who you are. Revalue yourself and they will confirm the change." **–Neville Goddard**

79. "Nothing comes from without; all things come from within - from the subconscious" **– Neville Goddard**

80. "Assume the feeling of your wish fulfilled and observe the route that your attention follows." **– Neville Goddard**

81. "Dare to believe in the reality of your assumption and watch the world play its part
relative to to its fulfillment."
–Neville Goddard

82. "It is always the false that makes you suffer, the false desires and fears, the false values and ideas, the false relationships between people. Abandon the false and you are free of pain; truth makes happy, truth liberates." – **Sri Nisargadatta Maharaj**

83. "Wisdom is knowing I am nothing, Love is knowing I am everything, and between the two my life moves." – **Nisargadatta Maharaj**

84. "Absolute perfection is here and now, not in some future, near or far. The secret is in action - here and now. It is your behavior that blinds you to yourself. Disregard whatever you think yourself to be and act as if you were absolutely perfect - whatever your idea of perfection may be. All you need is courage." – **Nisargadatta Maharaj**

85. "You see what you choose to see, because all perception is a choice. And when you cease to impose your meanings on what you see, your spiritual eyes will open, and you will see a world free of judgment and shining in its endless beauty." – **Paul Ferrini**

86. "To put it simply, you are never right to make wrong, or wrong to make right. To be right, make right." – **Paul Ferrini**

87. "You cannot experience joy in life by opposing the ideas or actions of other people. You can experience joy only by remaining faithful to the truth within your own heart. And this truth never rejects others, but invites them in." – **Paul Ferrini**

88. "Consciousness does not just passively reflect the objective material world; it plays an active role in creating reality itself." –**Stanislav Grof**

89. "The desire for perfection is that desire which always makes every pleasure appear incomplete, for there is no joy or pleasure so great in this life that it can quench the thirst in our soul." – **Stanislav Grof**

90. "This sense of perfection has a built-in contradiction, one that Ram Dass once captured very succinctly by a statement he had heard from his Himalayan guru: "The world is absolutely perfect, including your own dissatisfaction with it, and everything you are trying to do to change it." – **Stanislav Grof**

91. "With the courage of the soul, we don't focus only on self-preservation, security, or safety; in fact, such courage compels us to risk our comfort and safety, and sometimes even our lives, as we act according to our most deeply held values. This kind of valor comes from a higher source and is the necessary ingredient for us to create a different dream."
–**Alberto Villoldo**

92. "Unlike longings, hopes, or even concrete goals, these affirmations can manifest in every moment when you hold them in your heart.

Then you naturally and easily behave in accordance with your dream, accessing the tremendous power of courage." – **Alberto Villoldo**

93. "You recognize your connection to others and perceive that you aren't the only one who matters, and you genuinely care about the good of all of Earth's creatures." – **Alberto Villoldo**

94. "Be Impeccable With Your Word. Speak with integrity. Say only what you mean. Avoid using the word to speak against yourself or to gossip about others. Use the power of your word in the direction of truth and love. "

–**Miguel Ruiz**

95."Don't Take Anything Personally. Nothing others do is because of you. What others say and do is a projection of their own reality, their own dream. When you are immune to the opinions and actions of others, you won't be the victim of needless suffering."
– **Miguel Ruiz**

96. "Don't Make Assumptions. Find the courage to ask questions and to express what you really want. Communicate with others as clearly as you can to avoid misunderstandings, sadness and drama. With just this one agreement, you can completely transform your life." – **Miguel Ruiz**

97. " Always Do Your Best. Your best is going to change from moment to moment; it will be different when you are healthy as opposed to sick. Under any circumstance, simply do your best, and you will avoid self-judgment, self-abuse and regret." – **Don Miguel Ruiz**

98."Maturity does not always come with age; sometimes age comes alone." – **John C. Maxwell**

99."Quality is never an accident. It is always the result of intelligent effort." – **John Ruskin**

100."Sometimes questions are more important than answers." – **Nancy Willard**

101."Do you want to know who you are? Don't ask. Act! Action will delineate and define you." – **Thomas Jefferson**

102."Everyone thinks of changing the world, but no one thinks of changing himself. "– **Leo Tolstoy**

103."If a team intimidate you physically and you let them, they've won." – **Mia Hamm**

104. "Let your imagination release your imprisoned possibilities." – **Robert H. Schuller**

105. "There is no such thing as life in-between." – **Pat Riley**

106. "Be a yardstick of quality. Some people aren't used to an environment where excellence is expected. " – **Steve Jobs**

107. "Nothing is really work unless you would rather be doing something else." – **James M. Barrie**

108. "If you learn from defeat, you haven't really lost." – **Zig Ziglar**

109. "You are never too old to set another goal or to dream a new dream." – **C. S. Lewis**

110."Whatever you can do, or dream you can, begin it. Boldness has genius, power and magic in it." – **Johann Wolfgang von Goethe**

111."The more I want to get something done, the less I call it work." – **Richard Bach**

112."Many of life's failures are people who did not realize how close they were to success when they gave up." – **Thomas A. Edison**

113."Accept responsibility for your life. Know that it is you who will get you where you want to go, no one else." – **Les Brown**

114."The will to win is important, but the will to prepare is vital." – **Joe Paterno**

115."You can't build a reputation on what you are going to do." – **Henry Ford**

116."Whenever you do a thing, act as if all the world were watching." – **Thomas Jefferson**

117."Out of suffering have emerged the strongest souls; the most massive characters are seared with scars." – **Khalil Gibran**

118."You can never quit. Winners never quit, and quitters never win."– **Ted Turner**
119."The only limit to our realization of tomorrow will be our doubts of today." – **Franklin D. Roosevelt**

120."If you want to succeed you should strike out on new paths, rather than travel the worn paths of accepted success." – **John D. Rockefeller**

121."When you are asked if you can do a job, tell 'em, 'Certainly I can!' Then get busy and find out how to do it." – **Theodore Roosevelt**

122."Don't join an easy crowd; you won't grow. Go where the expectations and the demands to perform are high." – **Jim Rohn**

123."In the middle of every difficulty lies opportunity." – **Albert Einstein**

124."You have to do the work. You have to make the opportunity. It doesn't find you, you find it." – **Jared Leto**

125."For what it will make of you to achieve it." – **Jim Rohn**

126. "Be miserable. Or motivate yourself. Whatever has to be done, it's always your choice." – **Wayne Dyer**

127. "If you really want to do something, you'll find a way. If you don't, you'll find an excuse." – **Jim Rohn**

128. "The secret of getting ahead is getting started." – **Mark Twain**

129. "Winning is habit. Unfortunately, so is losing." – **Vince Lombardi**

130. "Success consists of going from failure to failure without loss of enthusiasm." – **Winston Churchill**

131."It ain't over 'til it's over." – **Yogi Berra**

132."I don't measure a man's success by how high he climbs but how high he bounces when he hits bottom." – **George S. Patton**

133."Always do more than is required of you." – **George S. Patton**

134."Being defeated is often a temporary condition. Giving up is what makes it permanent." – **Marilyn vos Savant**

135."For things to change, you have to change." – **Jim Rohn**

136. "Without a customer, you don't have a business – all you have is a hobby." – **Don Peppers**

137. "If we wait for the moment when everything, absolutely everything is ready, we shall never begin." – **Ivan Turgenev**

138. "The only thing that overcomes hard luck is hard work." – **Harry Golden**

139. "Only the mediocre are always at their best." – **Jean Giraudoux**

140. "Don't be afraid to give up the good to go for the great." – **John D. Rockefeller**

141."You can't live a perfect day without doing something for someone who will never be able to repay you." – **John Wooden**

142."I have no Napoleonic dream. I'm just hard-working and pragmatic." – **Roman Abramovich**

143."A successful man is one who can lay a firm foundation with the bricks others have thrown at him." – **David Brinkley**

144."Work hard at your job and you can make a living. Work hard on yourself and you can make a fortune." – **Jim Rohn**

145. "I'm not out there sweating for three hours every day just to find out what it feels like to sweat." – **Michael Jordan**

146. "Most people would like to be delivered from temptation but would like it to keep in touch." – **Robert Orben**

147. "An innovator is one who does not know it cannot be done." – **Raghunath Anant Mashelkar**

148. "It's not whether you get knocked down, it's whether you get up." – **Vince Lombardi**

149. "The only person you are destined to become is the person you decide to be." – **Ralph Waldo Emerson**

150."Take care of your body. It's the only place you have to live." – **Jim Rohn**

151."Motivation is the fuel, necessary to keep the human engine running." – **Zig Ziglar**

152."I am not a product of my circumstances. I am a product of my decisions." – **Stephen Covey**

153."Push yourself again and again. Don't give an inch until the final buzzer sounds." – **Larry Bird**

154. "Very often a change of self is needed more than a change of scene." – **A. C. Benson**

155. "The victory of success is half won when one gains the habit of work." – **Sarah T. Bolton**

156. "Look the world straight in the eye." – **Helen Keller**

157. "Nurture your mind with great thoughts, for you will never go any higher than you think." – **Benjamin Disraeli**

158. "You don't run 26 miles at five minutes a mile on good looks and a secret recipe." – **Frank Shorter**

159."To climb steep hills requires a slow pace at first." – **William Shakespeare**

160."A ship in port is safe, but that's not what ships are built for." – **Grace Hopper**

161."Nothing will ever be attempted if all possible objections must first be overcome." – **Samuel Johnson**

162."Leaders don't complain about what's not working. Leaders celebrate what is working and work to amplify it." – **Simon Sinek**

163."My advice is find fuel in failure. Sometimes failure gets you closer to where you want to be." – **Michael Jordan**

164."One of my rules is: Never TRY to do anything. Just do it." – **Ani DiFranco**

165."Someone is sitting in the shade today because someone planted a tree a long time ago." – **Warren Buffett**

166."Begin to be now what you will be hereafter." – **William James**

167."The future belongs to those who believe in the beauty of their dreams." – **Eleanor Roosevelt**

168."Someone's opinion of you does not have to become your reality." – **Les Brown**

169."If you don't feel you have something to prove every day, you'll never improve." – **Billy Donovan**

170."To accomplish great things, we must not only act, but also dream, not only plan, but also believe." – **Anatole France**

171."The great accomplishments of man have resulted from the transmission of ideas and enthusiasm." – **Thomas J. Watson**

172."The most valuable of all talents is that of never using two words when one will do." – **Thomas Jefferson**

173."Keep away from people who try to belittle your ambition." – **Mark Twain**

174."Good, Better, Best. Never let it rest. Until your Good is Better, and your Better is your Best." – **Tim Duncan**

175."I'll beat him so bad he'll need a shoehorn to put his hat on." – **Muhammad Ali**

176."It is not what they take away from you that counts. It's what you do with what you have left." – **Hubert H. Humphrey**

177. "If you can't do the little things right, you will never do the big things right." – **William H. McRaven**

178. "The ultimate inspiration is the deadline." – **Nolan Bushnell**

179. "If you're fail to prepare, you're prepared to fail." – **Mark Spitz**

180. "If opportunity doesn't knock, build a door." – **Milton Berle**

181. "Push YOURSELF to the edge of YOUR limits. That's how they expand." – **Robin Sharma**

182. "There's always a way – if you're committed." – **Tony Robbins**

183. "You cannot change your destination overnight, but you can change your direction overnight." – **Jim Rohn**

184. "Courage is resistance to fear, mastery of fear, not absence of fear." – **Mark Twain**

185. "After climbing a great hill, one only finds that there are many more hills to climb." – **Nelson Mandela**

186. "In matters of style, swim with the current; in matters of principle, stand like a rock." – **Thomas Jefferson**

187. "When you are afraid, do the thing you are afraid of and soon you will lose your fear of it." – **Norman Vincent Peale**

188. "The best way to predict the future is to create it." – **Peter Drucker**

189. "The only way to define your limits is by going beyond them." – **Arthur C. Clarke**

190."The great use of life is to spend it for something that will outlast it." – **William James**

191."The time to repair the roof is when the sun is shining." – **John F. Kennedy**

192."Knowing is not enough; we must apply. Willing is not enough; we must do." – **Johann Wolfgang von Goethe**

193."Action may not always bring happiness; but there is no happiness without action." – **Benjamin Disraeli**

194."It is easy to sit up and take notice, What is difficult is getting up and taking action." – **Honore de Balzac**

195."Laziness may appear attractive, but work gives satisfaction." – **Anne Frank**

196."You need to make a commitment, and once you make it, then life will give you some answers." – **Les Brown**

197."If we did all the things we are capable of doing, we would literally astound ourselves." – **Thomas A. Edison**

198."When you hear that something can't be done, ignore

that advice and push forward." – **Robert Kiyosaki**

199."The secret of joy in work is contained in one word – excellence. To know how to do something well is to enjoy it." – **Pearl S. Buck**

200."To live is the rarest thing in the world. Most people exist, that is all." – **Oscar Wilde**

201."There is no elevator to success, you have to take the stairs." – **Zig Ziglar**

202."The more you gripe about your problems, the more problems you have to gripe about!" – **Zig Ziglar**

203. "You see things, and you say, why?? But I dream things that never were, and I say? Why not?" – **George Bernard Shaw**

204. "Ninety-nine percent of the failures come from people who have the habit of making excuses." – **George Washington Carver**

205. "High achievement always takes place in the framework of high expectation." – **Charles Kettering**

206. "Concern yourself not with what you tried and failed in, but with what it is still possible for you to do." – **Pope John XXII**

207."Knowledge is proud that it knows so much; wisdom is humble that it knows no more." – **William Cowper**

208."All the world is full of suffering. It is also full of overcoming." – **Helen Keller**

209."Obstacles are what you see when you take your eyes off your goals." – **Brian Tracy**

210."What sculpture is to a block of marble, education is to the human soul." – **Joseph Addison**

211."Be a voice not an echo." – **Albert Einstein**

212. "Live out of your imagination, not your history." – **Stephen Covey**

213. "When love and skill work together, expect a masterpiece." – **John Ruskin**

214. "If you do what you've always done, you'll get what you've always gotten." – **Tony Robbins**

215. "It is in your moments of decision that your destiny is shaped." – **Tony Robbins**

216. "Unless you try to do something beyond what you have already mastered, you will never grow." – **Ralph Waldo Emerson**

217."God has given us two hands, one to receive with and the other to give with." – **Billy Graham**

218."Your talent is God's gift to you. What you do with it is your gift back to God." – **Leo Buscaglia**

219."The results you achieve will be in direct proportion to the effort you apply." – **Denis Waitley**

220."The most interesting things in life happen just on the other side of your comfort zone." – **Michael Hyatt**

221."Nothing really worth having comes quickly and easily. If it did, I doubt that we would ever grow." – **Eknath Easwaran**

222."Choose to be optimistic, it feels better." – **Dalai Lama**

223."We are what we repeatedly do. Excellence, then, is not an act, but a habit." – **Aristotle**

224."Believe in yourself. Trust the process. Change forever." – **Bob Harper**

225."Your most unhappy customers are your greatest source of learning." – **Bill Gates**

226."Your present circumstances don't determine where you can go;

they merely determine where you start." – **Nido R Qubein**

227."The successful man will profit from his mistakes and try again in a different way." – **Dale Carnegie**

228."You can't cross the sea merely by standing and staring at the water." – **Rabindranath Tagore**

229."Never, never, never give up." – **Winston Churchill**

230."When you know better you do better." – **Maya Angelou**

231."You will never 'find' time for anything. If you want time, you must make it." – **Charles Buxton**

232."The real risk is doing nothing." – **Denis Waitley**

233."Our greatest weakness lies in giving up. The most certain way to succeed is always to try just one more time." – **Thomas A. Edison**

234."The ladder of success is best climbed by stepping on the rungs of opportunity." – **Ayn Rand**

235."Your life does not get better by chance, it gets better by change." – **Jim Rohn**

236."A competitive world offers two possibilities. You can lose. Or, if you want to win, you can change." – **Lester Thurow**

237."The man on top of the mountain didn't fall there." – **Vince Lombardi**

238."Running is the greatest metaphor for life, because you get out of it what you put into it." – **Oprah Winfrey**

239."The only way you can be the best at something is to be the best you can be." – **Susan Beth Pfeffer**

240."Success is getting what you want. Happiness is wanting what you get." – **Dale Carnegie**

241."Put all excuses aside and remember this: YOU are capable." – **Zig Ziglar**

242."Nothing is an obstacle unless you say it is." – **Wally Amos**

243."Motivation is simple. You eliminate those who are not motivated." – **Lou Holtz**

244."I don't know the key to success, but the key to failure is trying to please everybody." – **Bill Cosby**

245."Only when we are no longer afraid do we begin to live." – **Dorothy Thompson**

246."There is little success where there is little laughter." – **Andrew Carnegie**

247."Finish each day and be done with it. You have done what you could. Learn from it... tomorrow is a new day." – **Ralph Waldo Emerson**

248."Success is predictable." – **Brian Tracy**

249."The more attention you pay an enemy, the stronger you make him. Be attentive, but don't be paranoiac." – **Paulo Coelho**

250."We must accept finite disappointment, but never lose infinite hope." – **Martin Luther King, Jr.**

251."When it is obvious that the goals cannot be reached, don't adjust the goals, adjust the action steps." – **Confucius**

252."Ideas without action are worthless." – **Harvey Mackay**

253."The highest reward for a person's toil is not what they get for it, but what they become by it." – **John Ruskin**

254."Goals are discovered, not made." – **Richard J. Foster**

255. "A light heart lives long." – **William Shakespeare**

256. "We cannot become what we need by remaining what we are." – **John C. Maxwell**

257. "Don't be afraid to be ambitious about your goals. Hard work never stops. Neither should your dreams." – **Dwayne Johnson**

258. "Aim for the moon. If you miss, you may hit a star." – **W. Clement Stone**

259. "I've failed over and over and over again in my life and that is why I succeed." – **Michael Jordan**

260."High expectations are the key to everything." – **Sam Walton**

261."Life's challenges are not supposed to paralyze you, they're supposed to help you discover who you are." – **Bernice Johnson Reagon**

262."Never give up. When your heart becomes tired, just walk with your legs – but move on." – **Paulo Coelho**

263."When I work fourteen hours a day, seven days a week, I get lucky." – **Armand Hammer**

264."If you change the way you look at things, the things you look at change." – **Wayne Dyer**

265."You're never a loser until you quit trying." – **Mike Ditka**

266."The common denominator for success is work." – **John D. Rockefeller**

267."A hero is one who knows how to hang on one minute longer." – **Novalis**

268."Don't waste yourself in rejection, nor bark against the bad, but chant the beauty of the good." – **Ralph Waldo Emerson**

269."Do all you can with what you have in the time you have in the place you are." – **Nkosi Johnson**

270."Times will change for the better when you change." – **Maxwell Maltz**

271."My mentor said, 'Let's go do it', not 'You go do it'. How powerful when someone says, 'Let's!" – **Jim Rohn**

272."We can't help everyone, but everyone can help someone." – **Ronald Reagan**

273."There is only one corner of the universe you can be certain of improving, and that's your own self." – **Aldous Huxley**

274. "Success is not measured by where you are in life, but the obstacles you've over come." – **Booker T. Washington**

275. "If one does not know to which port one is sailing, no wind is favourable." – **Seneca the Younger**

276. "Choose a job you love, and you will never have to work a day in your life." – **Confucius**

277. "If you're going through hell, keep going." – **Winston Churchill**

278. "You don't get paid for the hour. You get paid for the value you bring to the hour." – **Jim Rohn**

279. "A man who wants to lead the orchestra must turn his back on the crowd." – **Max Lucado**

280. "The present moment is all you ever have." – **Eckhart Tolle**

281. "As long as you think the problem is out there, that very thought is the problem ."– **Stephen Covey**

282. "Chop your own wood and it will warm you twice." – **Henry Ford**

283. "Being wrong is acceptable, but staying wrong is totally unacceptable." – **Jack D. Schwager**

284."Always bear in mind that your own resolution to succeed is more important than any other." – **Abraham Lincoln**

285."Creativity is your best makeup skill, don't be afraid to experiment." – **Pat McGrath**

286."Belief in oneself is one of the most important bricks in building any successful venture." – **Lydia M. Child**

287."Obstacles are those frightful things you see when you take your eyes off your goal." – **Henry Ford**

288."Don't let life discourage you; everyone who got where he is had to begin where he was." – **Richard L. Evans**

289."I'm playing; I'm here. I'm going to fight until they tell me they don't want me anymore." – **Steve Nash**

290."You never know how strong you are, until being strong is your only choice." – **Bob Marley**

291."Success is not final, failure is not fatal: it is the courage to continue that counts." – **Winston Churchill**

292. "You will never change your life until you change something you do daily." – **Mike Murdock**

293. "The greatest discovery of my generation is that a human being can alter his life by altering his attitudes." – **William James**

294. "As you think, so shall you become." – **Bruce Lee**

295. "Do not wait to strike till the iron is hot; but make it hot by striking." – **William Butler Yeats**

296. "Don't find fault, find a remedy." – **Henry Ford**

297."Things may come to those who wait, but only the things left by those who hustle." – **Abraham Lincoln**

298."The reward of a thing well done, is to have done it." – **Ralph Waldo Emerson**

299."Grind Hard, Shine Hard." – **Dwayne Johnson**

300."If what you're working for really matters, you'll give it all you've got." – Nido R Qubein

301."Man is so made that when anything fires his soul, impossibilities vanish." – **Jean de La Fontaine**

302. "Great minds discuss ideas; average minds discuss events; small minds discuss people." – **Eleanor Roosevelt**

303. "Surmounting difficulty is the crucible that forms character." – **Tony Robbins**

304. "Everything is hard before it is easy." – **Johann Wolfgang von Goethe**

305. "Change your thoughts and you change your world."
– **Norman Vincent Peale**

306."Every day is a gift from God. Learn to focus on the Giver and enjoy the gift!" – **Joyce Meyer**

307."Failure is the condiment that gives success its flavor." – **Truman Capote**

308."Practice the philosophy of continuous improvement. Get a little bit better every single day." – **Brian Tracy**

309."We don't see things as they are, we see them as we are." – **Anais Nin**

310."To have more than you've got, become more than you are." – **Jim Rohn**

311. "A well-spent day brings happy sleep." – **Leonardo da Vinci**

312. "Work consists of whatever a body is obliged to do. Play consists of whatever a body is not obliged to do." – **Mark Twain**

313. "You don't win by being good. You win with hard work and sacrifice. Without that, skill is just potential." – **Bobby Orr**

314. "Nothing teaches character better than generosity." – **Jim Rohn**

315. "If at first you don't succeed- try, try again. Don't think of it as failure. Think of it as timed-release success." – **Robert Orben**

316. "Remember: Rewards come in action, not in discussion." – **Tony Robbins**

317. "Change the changeable, accept the unchangeable, and remove yourself from the unacceptable." – **Denis Waitley**

318. "The person that said winning isn't everything, never won anything." – **Mia Hamm**

319. "If you keep saying things are going to be bad, you have a good chance of being a prophet." – **Isaac Bashevis Singer**

320. "When I go to the press conference before the game, in my mind the game has already started... " – **Jose Mourinho**

321. "Learn how to say no. Don't let your mouth overload your back." – **Jim Rohn**

322. "The happiness of your life depends upon the quality of your thoughts." – **Marcus Aurelius**

323. "I hear and I forget. I see and I remember. I do and I understand." – **Confucius**

324. "Every problem has in it the seeds of its own solution. If you don't have any problems, you don't get any seeds." – Norman **Vincent Peale**

325."The only limits to the possibilities in your life tomorrow are the buts you use today." – **Les Brown**

326."The only way to earn what you're really worth is to get paid based on your results." – **T. Harv Eker**

327."Life begins at the end of your comfort zone." – **Neale Donald Walsch**

328."You become what you believe." – **Oprah Winfrey**

329. "Tomorrow is the first blank page of a 365-page book. Write a good one." – **Brad Paisley**

330. "At one point in your life, you'll have the thing you want or the reasons why you don't." – **Andy Roddick**

331. "Genius is the ability to put into effect what is on your mind." – **F. Scott Fitzgerald**

332. "You cannot dream yourself into a character; you must hammer and forge yourself one." – **James Anthony Froude**

333. "Work joyfully and peacefully, knowing that right thoughts and right efforts inevitably bring about right results." – **James Allen**

334."Never retract, never explain, never apologize; get things done and let them howl." – **Nellie L. McClung**

335."You may be disappointed if you fail, but you are doomed if you don't try." – **Beverly Sills**

336."Our greatest glory is not in never falling, but in rising every time we fall." – **Confucius**

337."Flops are a part of life's menu and I've never been a girl to miss out on any of the courses." – **Rosalind Russell**

338. "When it's time to die, let us not discover that we have never lived." – **Henry David Thoreau**

339. "Some people want it to happen, some wish it would happen, others make it happen." – **Michael Jordan**

340. "I cannot always control what goes on outside. But I can always control what goes on inside." – **Wayne Dyer**

341. "To be a champ you have to believe in yourself when no one else will." – **Sugar Ray Robinson**

342."The difference between the impossible and the possible lies in a man's determination." – **Tommy Lasorda**

343."He who asks is a fool for five minutes, but he who does not ask remains a fool forever." – **Mark Twain**

344."Do what you can, with what you have, where you are." – **Theodore Roosevelt**

345."Exercise should be fun, otherwise, you won't be consistent." – **Laura Ramirez**

346."If a tree dies, plant another in its place." – **Carl Linnaeus**

347."Knowledge isn't power until it is applied." – **Dale Carnegie**

348."Success is often achieved by those who don't know that failure is inevitable." – **Coco Chanel**

349."If you don't love what you do, you won't do it with much conviction or passion." – **Mia Hamm**

350."Adopt the pace of nature: her secret is patience." – **Ralph Waldo Emerson**

351."Don't waste your energy trying to educate or change opinions... Do your thing and don't care if they like it. " – **Tina Fey**

352. "There is always room at the top." – **Daniel Webster**

353. "Ever tried. Ever failed. No matter. Try Again. Fail again. Fail better." – **Samuel Beckett**

354. "One chance is all you need." – **Jesse Owens**

355. "Expect problems and eat them for breakfast." – **Alfred Armand Montapert**

356. "Optimism is the faith that leads to achievement. Nothing can be done without hope and confidence." – **Helen Keller**

357. "Constant effort and frequent mistakes are the stepping stones to genius. " – **Elbert Hubbard**

358. "I race to win. If I am on the bike or in a car it will always be the same." – **Valentino Rossi**

359. "It's not the size of the dog in the fight, it's the size of the fight in the dog." – **Mark Twain**

360. "Shall we make a new rule of life from tonight: always to try to be a little kinder than is necessary?" – **James M. Barrie**

361. "Don't let your learning lead to knowledge. Let your learning lead to action." – **Jim Rohn**

362."Far too many people are looking for the right person, instead of trying to be the right person." – **Gloria Steinem**

363."What you think you become." – **Gautama Buddha**

364."Opportunities are usually disguised as hard work, so most people don't recognize them." – **Ann Landers**

365."A champion is someone who gets up when he can't." – **Jack Dempsey**

Hey there!!!

We hope you enjoyed our book. As a small family company, your feedback is very important to us. Please let us know how you like our book at:

believepublisher@gmail.com

Without your voice we don't exist!

Please, support us and leave a review!

Thank you!!!

www.ingramcontent.com/pod-product-compliance
Lightning Source LLC
LaVergne TN
LVHW010553070526
838199LV00063BA/4959